HOW TO GROW IN CHRIST

By Jack Kinneer

Presbyterian and Reformed Publishing Co.
Phillipsburg, New Jersey 08865

Printed in the United States of America
ISBN: 0-87552-284-X

CONTENTS

PREFACE

"Grow in the grace and knowledge of our Lord and Savior Jesus Christ."
—II Peter 3:18

Grass that ceases to grow, withers to a useless yellow-brown. The same is true for Christians. Unless they grow, their lives become stagnant and unproductive. Christians are not merely to remain at a standstill. Rather they are to grow, to mature and to ripen into the image of Jesus Christ. If God has made you His child in Christ, He wants you to progress in your faith from the toddler steps of first believing to the mature gait of ever-fuller conformity to His Son, Jesus. We are to grow in grace and knowledge, that is, in our experience of Christ's renewing mercy and in our intimate acquaintance with Him who is the source of all grace and life.

But how can I grow? What can I do? First, you must know that it is God alone who causes growth. You cannot do it yourself. "So neither he who plants nor he who waters is anything, but only God, who makes things grow" (I Corinthians 3:7). Yet God does use people. Some plant. Some water. You cannot grow by yourself; you need the help of other Christians whom God has equipped to plant and water, that is, to teach you the Word of God. You too must work. The command is addressed to you: "Grow in the grace and knowledge of . . . Christ." God, the Father, Son and Spirit, will supply the power, but you are to be active as well. God has given you His Word, the Bible, to instruct you in the path of maturity. "All Scripture is God-breathed and is useful for teaching, rebuking, correcting and training in righteousness, so that the man of God may be thoroughly equipped for every good work" (II Timothy 3:16-17).

This booklet is a guide to help you learn God's directions in the Bible. There are 12 lessons for you to complete by looking up passages in the Bible and answering questions. Each section of a lesson has a brief explanation of what you learned from the Bible to aid you in understanding and remembering what God has just taught you in his Word. If you are using this booklet as part of a study group, it is best to do each lesson at home beforehand and come to the group time ready to discuss and apply the truths learned. The New International Version of the Bible is recommended for use with this booklet because the study questions are taken from the exact wording of that translation. However, any reliable translation will work.

Remember do not just do the lessons—apply them to your life. "Do not merely listen to the Word, and so deceive yourselves. Do what it says" (James 1:22).

LESSON ONE: **HOW TO BE SURE YOU ARE A CHRISTIAN**

To grow in Christ you must first be in Christ. In other words, you must be a Christian. This first lesson is designed to help you know whether or not you are a Christian and how to become a Christian if you are not. Knowing Christ is the most important matter in all of life. Rejecting Christ is the most harmful. If you are a Christian and are sure you are, this lesson will be a helpful review. The apostles Paul and Peter considered it their duty to remind Christians of the basics (I Corinthians 15:1-5; II Peter 1:12-15).

I. Part One: *Jesus Christ and Your Need*

A. The Person and Work of Christ

1. Read Philippians 2:6-11.

a. Who is Jesus by nature? (v. 6)[1] ______________________

b. Jesus Christ, the Son of God, is one with the Father and the Holy Spirit as the only true and living God, and yet they are three distinct persons, equal in power and glory. The Father is not the Son. The Son is not the Spirit. Yet they are not three gods but one God. They are each fully God and together are the one true God. This mystery we call the Trinity.

c. What did God's Son become? (v. 7) ______________________

d. How far did Jesus go in His humiliation and obedience? (v. 8)

____

1. The phrase "form of God" (in some translations) means "in very nature God" (NIV).

e. What did God the Father do in response to Jesus' obedience? (v. 9)

____

____

f. What will every person do eventually? (vv. 10-11)______________

2. Read I Corinthians 15:3-7.

a. For what did Jesus die? ______________________________

b. Did He remain in the grave? __________________________

c. Did people see Jesus alive after His burial? ______________

Jesus is no ordinary man. He is true God who became true man. In one person Jesus is both God and man. As a man, Jesus came to save His people by doing for them what they could not do for themselves. We had disobeyed God, broken His law and earned His punishment. Jesus, however, perfectly obeyed His Father. He never sinned. Moreover, He willingly endured the punishment His people deserved for their sin. As their substitute, He satisfied God's just requirement that sin be punished by taking their punishment on Himself. In this way God is both *just,* because sin is punished, and *merciful,* because He forgives the sins of His people. Because of Jesus' perfect obedience to the Father, God raised Him bodily from the dead and seated Him at His right hand. Jesus now reigns as the Lord of all and rules the world to defeat His and His people's enemies.

B. Your Need for Christ

1. Read Romans 3:23.

a. How many people have sinned? ______________________

b. Are you a sinner? ______________________________

2. Read Romans 6:23.

a. What is the wage of sin? __________________________

b. What is God's free gift? __________________________

c. Through whom does this gift come?____________________

3. Read Romans 2:6-11.

   a. What will God judge us by? (v. 6) ______________________

   b. What will happen to evil people? (vv. 8-9)______________________

   ____

   c. What are the characteristics of those who will be punished? (v.8)

   ____

   ____

   d. Do these characteristics describe you (before you became a Christian)? ______________________

We are all sinners, that is, we are rebels against God. Perhaps you do not think you are much of a sinner. Try this experiment. Read the Ten Commandments (Exodus 20:1-17). How many of these commandments have you outwardly broken? How many have you broken in your thoughts? If you are honest, you will have to admit you have broken either by actions or thoughts every commandment. That makes you a very lawless person. Now do you see why God takes your sin so seriously? God will punish us for our sin with the troubles of this life, with physical death and with the sufferings of hell forever. That is why we need Jesus.

II. Part Two: *God's Promise and Your Response*

A. God Promises Eternal Life

1. Read John 6:40.

   a. What does Jesus promise?______________________

   ____

   ____

   b. What must you do? ______________________

2. Read Romans 10:9-13.

   a. What two things must you do? (v. 9) ______________________

b. What will be the result? (v. 10)________________

c. If you call on Christ to save you, what will happen? (v. 13)______

Faith in Christ means you trust Him to save you and you submit to Him as Lord. If you just want forgiveness but do not want Christ as *your* Lord, then you do not have real faith. True faith expresses itself in the statement, "Jesus is Lord." The person who says he believes in Christ but does not begin to obey Christ (that is, stop sinning) is fooling himself (I John 2:3-6). Faith always has with it a desire to turn from sin and to serve Christ. True faith brings true repentance. You must rely on Christ to forgive you and to change you (see B. 4 below).

B. The Gratitude We Owe to God for Salvation

1. Read John 14:15; 15:12.

   a. What will you do if you love Jesus? ________________

   b. Whom should you love most?________________

   c. What is Jesus' command? (15:12)________________

2. Read Matthew 22:37-39.

   a. How much should you love God?________________

   b. Whom else should you love? ________________

c. How should you love your neighbor? ______________________

3. Read II Corinthians 5:14-15.

a. What should compel us? ______________________

b. Why should it compel us? ______________________

____

c. Whom should we live for? ______________________

____

d. Whom should we *not* live for? ______________________

4. Read Ephesians 2:8-10.

a. Are you saved by your good works? ______________________

b. How are you saved? ______________________

c. Why? ______________________

____

d. What is the role of good works? (v. 10) ______________________

____

e. What were you created for? ______________________

____

Here is a good way to remember this truth from Ephesians 2:8-10. "We are not saved by our works but we are saved to work." Christ alone can save. We receive Him and His salvation by faith alone. However, our faith in Christ must produce a desire to obey Christ. We do not obey hoping to be saved, but we obey knowing that we are already saved by Christ. Even the good works we do as Christians are possible only because God has saved us. We are created in Christ for good works. Apart from Him we cannot please God (John 15:4-6). As a matter of fact, our good works themselves are sufficiently tainted by our sin that they are not acceptable to God in themselves, but God is pleased to accept and reward them for the sake of Christ and His perfect righteousness (Isaiah 64:6;

I Peter 2:5). Good works are only those deeds that are done according to God's law and are done out of a heart full of faith in Christ. We are free from the law as it condemns us for sin, but the law ever remains God's standard by which we are to measure our lives (Romans 8:1-4).

C. The Benefits of Being a Christian

1. Read Colossians 2:13.

a. What were you? ______________________________

b. What has God done to you? ______________________________

____

c. How many of your sins has He forgiven? ______________________________

2. Read Galatians 4:4-7.

a. Why did Christ redeem us? (v. 5) ______________________________

____

b. What are you? (v. 6) ______________________________

c. Whom has God sent into our hearts? ______________________________

d. What does the Spirit teach us to say? ______________________________

3. Reread John 6:40.

a. What two things does Jesus promise? ______________________________

____

____

b. Will death be the end of you? ______________________________

God has made us alive. That means all our sins are forgiven and we are at peace with God. In fact, God adopts us as His sons. He sends the Holy Spirit into our hearts so we will know we are sons. The Spirit is the one who empowers us to live for Christ. Even when we die, our souls go to be with Jesus. Then when Christ returns, our bodies will be raised and we will live forever with Christ on a renewed earth (II Peter 3:13).

LESSON TWO: **HOW TO PRAY**

Prayer is talking with God. When we talk to other people we like to know something about them: their names, ages or occupations. So then, if we are to enjoy prayer we must know something about God and what He is like. Prayer is both very simple and very difficult. It is simple because it is talking with our heavenly Father. It is difficult because our sin makes us uncomfortable near God. But prayer is too important to ignore. It is the life blood of being a Christian. A Christian who never prays is like a son who never speaks to his father.

I. Part One: *What Is God Like?*

There is much to learn about God. We can only cover a few areas in this study. We will look at three parts of God's character that will help us understand our relationship to Him.

A. God Is Sovereign (All-Powerful and in Control).

1. Read Jeremiah 32: 17, 27.

a. What did God make?________________________________

b. Does anything exist that God did not make?______________

c. Is there anything too hard for God to do? ________________

2. Read Isaiah 46:10-11.

a. How much of what God desires to do will He do? __________

b. Can anyone frustrate God's plan?________________________

3. Read Psalm 24:1.

a. How much of the world does God own?___________________

b. Does God own you? ___________________________________

c. List some things that God owns. ______

______

______

______

______

4. Reflection
   a. What does God's sovereignty teach you about why you should pray? ______

______

______

______

______

   b. Does God have enough power to answer prayer? ______

B. God Is Holy (Pure and Righteous).

1. Read Psalm 5:4-6.

   a. What does God not take pleasure in? ______

   b. Where can the wicked not dwell? ______

   c. What is God's attitude to those who do wrong? ______

______

2. Read I Peter 1:13-15.

   a. What is God's character like? ______

   b. Why should we also be holy? ______

______

3. Reflection

   a. What does God's holiness teach you about why you should pray?

b. What should you always remember to ask for when you pray because God is holy?

C. God Is Loving (Merciful, Kind, Gracious).

1. Read Romans 5:8.

a. Does God love sinners?

b. How did God show His love?

2. Read Romans 9:14-18.

a. Who decides whom God will love?

b. Does God love us because of what we do?

c. Why does He have mercy on us?

3. Reflection

a. What does God's mercy teach you about why you should pray?

b. Do you think God is willing to hear the prayers of His people?

Prayer is significant because of who God is. He is all-powerful, and so He can answer our prayers. Actually, His power is so great He actually leads us to pray for the things He has already determined to do. God is holy, and so we must always approach God asking His forgiveness and trusting in His Son who died for us. God is merciful, and so He eagerly listens to and answers our prayers even when His answer is "No! I have something else for you."

II. Part Two: *What Is Prayer?*

Prayer means talking with God. When we pray we should be careful to include three things: praise, confession of sin, and requests.

A. Praise: Read Romans 11:33-36.

1. What is Paul doing? ______________________________

2. For what does Paul praise God? ______________________________

____

3. Can you think of some things to praise God for? (Think about part I on what God is like.) ______________________________

____

____

____

(Now take a minute and praise Him. Just say: "God, I thank you because. . . .")

B. Confession of Sin: Read Psalm 32:3-5.

1. What is the psalmist's problem? ______________________________

____

2. What did he do? ______________________________

3. What was God's response? ______________________________

4. Do you have any sins to confess to God? Make a list right now. ______

____

____

Now say to God, "God, I'm sorry I did. . . . Please forgive me for Jesus' sake."

5. What characteristic of God gives you confidence He will forgive you? ____________________

C. Petition (Asking God for Things You or Others Need)

1. Read Luke 11:2-4.

   a. What should you pay for? (5 things) ____________________

   ____

   ____

   ____

   ____

   b. What are you asking when you pray "Your name be hallowed"?

   ____

   ____

   c. What are you asking when you pray for daily bread? ____________________

   ____

2. Read Luke 11:5-10.

   a. Should you give up praying if God does not *seem* to answer at first? ____________________

   b. Will God answer you? ____________________

3. Read James 1:5-8.

   a. What must you do when you pray? ____________________

   b. What must you not do? ____________________

   c. What is a person like who doubts? ____________________

   ____

   d. Should a doubting person think God will answer? ____________________

(If you doubt, confess your sin to God, for doubt is sin. Then ask God to help you believe. Also read God's Word, which helps you to believe—Romans 10:17.)

e. How does God's sovereignty relate to your boldness in asking God to meet your needs and others' needs? ______________________

____

____

III. Part Three: *Practical Helps on How to Pray*

A. Pick a special time each day when you can be alone to pray.

B. Begin by praising God, then confess your sins, and then tell God your needs. Be sure to pray for others also!

C. It is helpful to make lists. Make one list of things for which to praise and thank God. Make a second list of people and things for which to ask God's help. It is often helpful to arrange these lists into daily groups. You might want to begin by using this chart.

PRAISES	REQUESTS
Monday	
1.	1.
2.	2.
3.	3.
Tuesday	
1.	1.
2.	2.
3.	3.

Wednesday	
1.	1.
2.	2.
3.	3.
Thursday	
1.	1.
2.	2.
3.	3.
Friday	
1.	1.
2.	2.
3.	3.
Saturday	
1.	1.
2.	2.
3.	3.
Sunday	
1.	1.
2.	2.
3.	3.

Remember, it is proper to pray repeatedly for someone or something; so each day's list does not have to be unique. If you can think of only one request, that is enough to start. As you grow in your faith, your lists will get longer.

D. Do not worry about how "pretty" your prayer is. God cares about your sincerity and faith. He knows what's on your mind even if you cannot express it.

E. Ask God to help you pray. He will!

F. Find another Christian who will pray with you perhaps once a week.

LESSON THREE: **HOW TO LIVE BY THE POWER OF THE HOLY SPIRIT**

When God saved you, He did not leave you all alone to live the Christian life in your own strength. Actually, the Christian life is impossible. But God's power can do the impossible, that is, enable you to live the Christian life. This section is about the work of God's Holy Spirit who gives us power to live as Christ's disciples. The Holy Spirit is the third person of the Trinity. He, with God the Son and God the Father, is the one true and living God. In the Bible the Holy Spirit is called "the Spirit of Christ," "the Spirit of God," and simply "the Spirit."

I. Part One: *What the Holy Spirit Does*

A. He Unites Us to Jesus (Conversion).

1. Read I Corinthians 12:3.

a. What can a person not do if he does not have the Spirit? ________

____

b. Can you become a Christian without the Spirit?________________

c. What can you not do if you have the Spirit? __________________

____

2. Read I Corinthians 12:12-13.

a. How are we united to Christ's body? ______________________

____

b. Is this true for every Christian?______________________________

3. Read Ephesians 3:16-17.

a. For what does Paul pray? ___________________________________

____

b. What is the result of the Spirit's work? ______________________

____

The Spirit unites us to Jesus by causing us to believe. Faith is God's gift that the Holy Spirit gives through the hearing and reading of God's Word (Philippians 1:29; Romans 10:17; II Thessalonians 2:13). The Spirit is the bond that makes us belong to Jesus (Romans 8:9). Every Christian is baptized with the Holy Spirit, that is, Christ pours out the Spirit on us and so unites us to Himself by that Spirit. By the Spirit, Christ ever lives in us. It is the Spirit who communicates to us Christ and all His benefits.

B. He Assures Us (The Witness of the Spirit).

1. Read Romans 8:15-16.

a. What is the Spirit called? (v. 15) ______________________

____

b. What does He enable us to do? (v. 15) ______________________

____

c. About what does the Spirit testify? (v. 16) ______________________

____

2. Read Ephesians 1:13-14.

a. What is the seal that God has given you? (v. 13) ______________

____

b. What else is the Spirit called? (v. 14) ______________________

c. What does He guarantee? ______________________

____

(Our inheritance = resurrection and life eternal.)

The Spirit not only unites us to Jesus; He assures us that we belong to God. The Spirit teaches us to call God, "Father." The Spirit is God's seal of ownership on us and our guarantee of complete salvation. Since the Spirit is almighty no one can ever remove the Spirit from us. Not even

Satan has that power. This is one reason why a person who is a true Christian cannot lose his salvation. Who has the power to take the Spirit away from us? The Holy Spirit is the sovereign God.

C. The Spirit Renews Us to Be Like Jesus (Sanctification).

1. Read II Corinthians 3:17-18.

a. Where is there freedom? ______________________________

______________(This freedom is freedom from sin.)

b. Whom are we being changed to be like?______________________

c. Who does the transforming? ____________________________

2. Read Galatians 5:22.

a. List the things the Spirit produces in us: ____________________

____

____

b. Do you see any of these in your life? ____________________

c. Try to make a list of the opposites of the fruit of the Spirit. ______

____

____

3. Read Romans 8:9.

a. Who controls you? ______________________________

b. What does not control you?____________________________

The Spirit makes us to be like Jesus. He does this by creating in us such qualities as love and patience. He empowers us to stop sinning. We can do what pleases God because the Spirit gives us power. He is our life and our strength. That is why we must not ignore the Spirit or try to live without depending on Him. The Spirit's work in making us like Jesus continues throughout our earthly life and is completed at the resurrection when even our bodies are transformed to be like Christ's body (Philippians 3:20-21).

II. Part Two: *How to Live by the Spirit*

A. Being Filled by the Spirit

1. Read Galatians 5:25.

   a. Who gives us life?______________________________

   b. What are we to do? ______________________________

   ____

   c. Should we sit idly waiting for the Spirit to do something? ______

2. Read Ephesians 5:18.

   a. What are we not to do? ______________________________

   b. What are we to do? ______________________________

   c. What does it mean to be filled?[1] ______________________________

   ____

   ____

B. How to Live by the Spirit

Being filled with or keeping in step with the Spirit sounds very mysterious. Actually it means that we submit to and rely on the Spirit. We look to Him for help. This means faith and prayer.

1. Read Galatians 2:20.

   a. Who is your true life? ______________________________

   b. How does Christ live in you? ______________________________

   ______________(See also Romans 8:9.)

   c. How are you to live? ______________________________

2. Reread Ephesians 3:16-17.

---

1. (Filled = controlled and empowered.)

a. What does Paul pray for? ______________________________

____

____

____

b. Do you think you should pray this prayer for yourself? ________

______________How often? ______________________

c. Right now ask God to fill you and strengthen you by the Spirit.

Living by the Spirit does not mean life will be easy. Rather, the Spirit will make us to war continually with our sinful nature (Galatians 5:16-17). Spirit-filled people are people who suffer and struggle and yet in the midst of the battle are able to rejoice in Christ and live like Him. To keep in step with the Spirit you should daily ask God to strengthen you by the Spirit. Be willing to follow His lead. The Holy Spirit will never lead you to do anything contrary to God's Word. He always works in and through the Word. In fact, He is the author of the Bible (II Peter 1:21). To be filled with the Spirit and to have Christ's Word dwell in you (Colossians3:16) mean the same thing. To live by the Spirit you must live by the Word and to live by the Word you must live by faith. Reread Ephesians 3:16-17. It is a model for how you should pray daily for yourself. Study God's Word. Depend on God to help you obey, and begin to obey. This is what it means to be filled with the Spirit. The Spirit's power will be displayed in our lives as we trust Him and begin to obey His Word.

LESSON FOUR: **HOW TO PROFIT FROM THE BIBLE**

The Bible is God's Word. Apart from the Bible we cannot know Jesus Christ or serve Him. The Bible is the book that feeds us, teaches us, rebukes us and shows us Jesus. If you want to grow in your faith in Jesus then you must read and study the Bible. Paul writes to the Thessalonians, "And we also thank God continually because, when you received the word of God, which you heard from us, you accepted it not as the word of men, but as it actually is, the word of God, which is at work in you who believe" (I Thessalonians 2:13). We too need to receive the Word of God as God's very word to us, His people.

I. Part One: *What the Bible Is*

A. The Bible's Author

1. Read II Timothy 3:16.

a. Who gave the Bible?[1] ________________________

b. How much of the Bible comes from God? ______________

____

2. Read II Peter 1:20-21.

a. Did men come up with the Bible on their own? __________

b. What was the human writer's role? ________________

____

c. What was the Holy Spirit's role? _________________

____

---

1. "Scripture" is the Bible's name for itself.

The words of the Bible are both the words of its human authors and the very words of God. The Holy Spirit so worked in men by a variety of methods that the words the human writers chose were precisely the words God wanted used to express His message accurately. The result is that the Bible is authoritative because it is God speaking. It is infallible in all it teaches because God is perfect. It is completely sufficient for our needs because God is all-wise. But it is also understandable for God was pleased to speak to us in human words.

B. The Bible's Subject

1. The Bible has many different kinds of literature. There are books of history, poems, laws and letters.

2. But the Bible has *one theme:* Read Luke 24: 44-47.

   a. Who is the subject of the Bible? ______________________________

   b. What are the basic things the Bible tells us about Jesus?

   ____

   ____

Though the Bible is a complex book that can bewilder the first-time reader, it is a unified book with one central theme—Jesus Christ. The Bible is divided into two parts: the Old Testament and the New Testament. The Old Testament (or old covenant) tells us of God's dealings with His people in preparation for the coming of His Son into the world. The Old Testament prepares and prophesies the coming of Christ. The New Testament (or new covenant) records the deeds and words of Christ and gives us God's own interpretation of the significance of Christ. Together the Old and New Testaments form God's all-sufficient Word to us His people.

C. The Bible's Purpose

1. Read Romans 10:17.

   What does Christ's Word produce? ______________________________

2. Read II Timothy 3:15-17.

   a. What is the Bible for? (v. 16) ______________________________

   ____

____

b. What is the result of Bible study? (vv. 15, 17)_______________

____

_______________(compare Acts 20:32)

c. Can you be a thoroughly equipped Christian without the Bible?

____

The great purpose of the Bible is to bring us to faith in Christ and to cause us to grow up to maturity in Him. The Bible is totally adequate to do this. A Christian who has no interest in the Bible is one who cares little for Christ and His purposes.

II. Part Two: *How the Bible Is to Be Used*

The message of the Bible comes to us in three basic ways: We hear it preached by ministers of the gospel; we see it portrayed in baptism and the Lord's Supper;[2] we study the Bible as individuals and groups. We must not neglect any of these ways of being fed by God's Word.

A. Public Preaching

1. Read Romans 10:13-17.

a. Why is preaching necessary? (v. 14)_______________

____

b. What is the outcome of preaching? (v. 17)_______________

____

2. Read I Timothy 4:13-16.

a. What is a minister to do? (v. 13)_______________

____

____

2. You may know the Lord's Supper by names like "communion" or "eucharist."

b. What is he to watch closely? (v. 16) ____________________

____

c. What is the result of his preaching? (v. 16) ____________________

____

Be sure you regularly attend a church where the Bible is faithfully preached. Come ready to hear God's Word and to believe and obey. But be careful—there are many churches where the Bible is not faithfully preached (Acts 20:29). God Himself has established that preaching should be the basic means of conferring His salvation on His people. A minister preaches with a special authority because he is specially appointed and equipped to bring God's Word to His people. As long as the minister preaches from the Bible, what he says, God says; and so to reject the preacher's message is to reject God's Word.

B. Baptism and the Lord's Supper

Christ has instituted these visible signs to show us His grace and to seal us in His love. We call them a "visible word." In baptism and the Lord's Supper God himself preaches to us, not with human words, but with physical symbols. They are signs that point us to Christ and His benefits. They are seals that confirm God's grace to us in Christ. Just like the preached Word, they communicate God's grace to us as we see and believe.

1. Baptism[3]

a. Read Luke 3:16.

(1) What does baptism with water signify? ____________________

____

(2) Water baptism is a sign of the Holy Spirit baptism. In water baptism, water is poured on our heads. At conversion to Christ, the Holy Spirit is poured out upon us (Acts 2:17, 33; 10:47-48; I Corinthians 12:13).

3. To be baptized means to merge with, to be identified with or to be overwhelmed by, to be washed.

b. Read Romans 6:3-5.

(1) What does Holy Spirit baptism do? ____________________

____

____

(2) To whom are we united in Spirit baptism? ____________________

____

(3) Holy Spirit baptism unites us to Jesus and causes us to share in His salvation. Jesus died for us, and therefore when we are united to Him we share in the power of His death and die to our old sinful selves. We also live a new life, for we share in His resurrection life. Water baptism is God's outward seal of our incorporation into Christ and our share in all His benefits.

c. Read Acts 2:38.

(1) What special benefit is connected with water baptism in this passage? ____________________

(2) What else is mentioned besides baptism? ____________________

(3) To whom is the promise (sealed by baptism) given?[4] ____________________

____

Baptism has no power apart from true faith and repentance.[5] The mere pouring of water cleanses only the body. Christ alone can remove sins. However, baptism is not without meaning or power. In baptism Christ says to us: "As surely as this water cleanses your body so surely does my blood and Spirit cleanse you from your sins." Adults are baptized when they believe. But children of believers are baptized as infants according to God's promise (Acts 2:39) and are then called by that baptism to trust in Christ as they grow older.

---

4. Children of Christians are baptized to show they belong to Christ according to this promise.

5. Nonetheless, children of believers are baptized according to God's promise that He will grant faith and repentance to His people.

2. The Lord's Supper

a. Read I Corinthians 11:23-29.

(1) What do the bread and wine symbolize? (vv. 23-25) ________

____

(2) Why should we celebrate the Supper? (vv. 23-25) ________

____

(3) What do we proclaim by the meal? (v. 26) ________

____

(4) What must we do before we eat? (v. 28) ________

____

(5) What must we recognize when we eat? (v. 29) ________

____

b. Read I Corinthians 10:16-17.

(1) In what do we participate when we in faith eat and drink? (v. 16) ________

(2) What is the result of sharing the one meal? (v. 17) ________

____

The Lord's Supper recalls us to Christ crucified for us. In the Supper Christ teaches us with bread and wine that feed our *bodies* to look to Him who feeds our *souls* for eternal life. The Supper summons us to continually receive and rely on Christ as the only source of salvation and life. In the Supper we really partake of Christ, not by the physical eating but by faith. In the Supper the Lord says to us: "As surely as this bread and wine nourish your body so surely do my body and blood, crucified for you, feed and nourish you to eternal life." When we drink from the cup and eat the bread we ought to lift our hearts to heaven and fix our minds upon Christ (John 6:39-64).

C. Private Bible Study

1. Read Colossians 3:16.

a. What are you to let the Word do? ______________________

____

b. What are you to do as a result? ______________________

____

2. Read Acts 17:11.

a. What did the Bereans do in response to Paul's teaching? ________

____

b. Why did they examine the Scriptures? ________________

____

c. Do you think you should imitate their practice? __________

3. Read II Timothy 3:15.

a. What did Timothy know from youth?__________________

b. What was the outcome of knowing the Scriptures? _________

____

III. Part Three: *Some Practical Helps in Private Bible Study*

A. Use a modern translation such as the New International Version.

B. Set aside a special time each day to read the Bible when you are alone and are not likely to be disturbed.

C. Follow a plan. Usually a Bible study booklet like this one is a good way to start. You will also want to "just" read the Bible to become familiar with its contents.

D. When you don't understand something, write down your question and ask your pastor or Christian leader.

E. At the end of this booklet are some suggestions about books to help you with your Bible reading, and some thoughts on how to do Bible study.

LESSON FIVE: **HOW TO OVERCOME SIN—FORGIVENESS**

Christians are at war with sin. We are to cease sinning and begin obeying God. That is no easy task. It is a struggle that lasts the length of our earthly life. Sin has two aspects: guilt and power. The guilt of sin needs to be forgiven and the power of sin broken. The guilt of sin has to do with sin as viewed by the law. When a person breaks the law (sins) he becomes guilty. That means he is held responsible for his action, and he is liable to whatever punishment the law requires. The guilt of sin means we are liable to the punishment God deems appropriate to our crimes. In this lesson we will learn about forgiveness for our guilt.

I. Part One: *What Sin Is and Does*

A. The Nature of Sin

1. Read I John 3:4.

a. Define sin: ____________________

b. What is God's standard that shows us our sin? ____________________

c. Where can you find a summary of God's law?[1] ____________________

____

2. Read James 2:10-11.

a. Does one little sin matter? ____________________

b. How much of the law must you keep to not be a lawbreaker?

____

B. The Outcome of Sin

1. Read Nahum 1:2-3.

---

1. Exodus 20:1-17

a. What is God's attitude to sinners? ______________________

____

b. What is God slow to do? ______________________

c. What will he not leave undone? ______________________

____

2. Read Isaiah 59:2.

a. What does sin do? ______________________

____

b. Will God listen to sinners? ______________________

Sin is the violation of God's law. Anytime we do not obey perfectly the law of God we sin. We are guilty of law-breaking. The guilt of our sin separates us from God. God holds us accountable and as judge pronounces the sentence, "Condemned." Our sin angers God. We are his enemies. Even if we could change our present behavior we cannot erase our past record. God's own just nature requires that our sins be punished. This situation we call spiritual death, that is, separation from God. As condemned sinners we are liable to all the sufferings of this life, to physical death and to the pains of hell forever. However, in Christ, God has made peace by forgiving our guilt. This is called justification. In justification God deals with the guilt of our sin.

II. Part Two: *God's Solution to Our Guilt*

A. Christ's Work for Us: The Basis of Justification

1. Read I John 2:1-2.

a. Who speaks in our defense when we sin? ______________________

b. What has Jesus done for our sins? ______________________

____

c. What is an atoning sacrifice? (propitiation) ______________________

____

2. Read Galatians 3:10-14.

a. Who are under a curse? (v. 10) ______________________

____

b. How much of the law must you break to be under a curse? (v. 10)

____

c. How can no one be justified? (v. 11)______________________

____

d. What did Christ do to redeem us from the curse of the law? (v. 13)

____

____

(Curse = the law's punishment. The curses of the law are all the punishments prescribed by the law for law-breakers—Deuteronomy 28.)

An atoning sacrifice means that Christ died in our place (sacrifice) and paid for our sins (atonement) so that God does not need to be angry with us. Our sin is the cause of God's anger. His justice demands that sin be punished. If He did not punish sin he would deny Himself. God provided Christ to be punished in our place, to pay for our sins and so remove the reason for God's just anger. Jesus' death allows God to be both perfectly just (sin is punished) and merciful (we are forgiven). Jesus' death (actually all His sufferings and His sinless life) satisfies the demands of God's law. Jesus is perfectly righteous. His perfect righteousness includes His active obedience of God's law throughout His life and His enduring the penalty of the law in His death. Thus Christ's death is a "penal satisfaction," it satisfies the demands of God's law perfectly (Galatians 3:13). The law cursed us. Jesus took the law's curse for us.

B. Our Forgivenss or Justification by Faith

1. Read II Corinthians 5:18-21.

a. Through whom did God reconcile[2] us to Himself? (v. 18) ______

2. Reconcile = to make peace.

b. How did He reconcile us? (v. 18) ______

______

c. Did Jesus ever sin? (v. 21) ______

d. What happened to our sin? ______

______

(This means Jesus took responsibility for our sin and paid for it.)

e. What do we become?[3] ______

God accounts our sin to Christ who pays its penalty. God accounts Christ's sinlessness to us so that we are righteous. This is called imputation. The result is "justification."

2. Read Romans 3:19-28.

a. Can you define "justify"? ______

______

______

______(if not, see note below[4]).

b. Can you be declared righteous (justified) by keeping the law (vv. 19-20) ______

c. Why? (v. 23) ______

d. What did Jesus do so we could be justified? (v. 25) ______

______

e. What must we do? (vv. 22, 28) ______

---

3. Righteousness = perfect law-keeping or not sinning.

4. "Justify" means the same as "acquit." It is a judge's pronouncement that a person is not guilty of law-breaking. To be justified is to be declared righteous.

f. What does God give us? (vv. 21-22) ______________________

______________________ (Christ takes our sins and gives us His righteousness.)

3. Read Romans 5:1.

a. What is the result of justification? ______________________

b. Through whom is justification? ______________________

Jesus paid for our sins. God puts our guilt (bad record) to Jesus' account. God gives us the credit for Christ's perfect obedience (righteousness). God says to us, "acquitted" or "justified." This means all our sins are forgiven and we now are at peace with God. God no longer looks at us as enemies but as righteous. Once we are justified (declared righteous) we can never be condemned. This is because the righteousness that is the basis of God's verdict is not our own but Christ's. Christ paid for our sins and kept God's law for us. Christ's obedience or righteousness includes both His dying for our sins and His living a sinless life. This becomes ours by faith. Memorize the following question and answer so that you can remember this truth. "What is justification? Justification is an act of God's free grace, wherein He pardons all our sins and accepts us as righteous in His sight, only for the righteousness of Christ imputed to us, and received by faith alone."[5]

III. Part Three: *Dealing with Sin as a Christian*

If we are believers, God no longer counts our sins against us. We are justified once and for all. The sins we commit as Christians do not bring us into a state of legal condemnation. We are always righteous despite our sin because our righteousness is not ours but Christ's, which God reckons to our account. Once justified (acquitted) always justified (acquitted). However, our sins as Christians interfere with our fellowship with God. God does not want us to ignore our sin and so think He is unconcerned about how we live. Rather our sin grieves God and ruins our fellowship with Him (Ephesians 4:29). When we sinned as non-Christians, God as judge condemned us. When we sin as Christians, God our Father is offended. Like a human father, God is displeased with His sons' and daughters' misbehavior. He may punish them

---

5. Westminster Shorter Catechism, Question 33 (tense endings have been modernized).

so they will stop sinning. He will not cast them away because He is their Father. However, God has a simple solution to our sin.

A. Confess Our Sins

1. Read I John 1:8-9.

a. What happens if we say we do not sin? (v. 8) ________________

____

____

b. What should we do when we sin? (v. 9) ________________

____

c. What will God do when we confess to Him our sins? (v. 9) ________

____

____

____

d. Why will God do these things? ________________________

____

2. Read Psalm 32:2-5.

a. What happened when the psalmist kept silent? (vv. 3-4) ________

____

b. Was the psalmist a joyful person? ________________________

c. Did God discipline him? (v. 4) ________________________

d. What did the psalmist do to solve his problem? (v. 5) ________

____

e. What did God do? ________________________________

____

Sin should not be left to fester. Confess your sin and ask God to forgive you. He promises He will. Christ is praying for you! Satan has two tricks he will try on you. He will try to make you think that because you sinned, God must hate you and will no longer accept you. That is not true. You are once for all at peace with God. You are justified even of the sins you will commit in the future. Your sin as a Christian does not condemn you, but it does bring you under God's fatherly discipline. Second, Satan will try to cause you to think lightly of sin, to pretend it really is not sin. That also is a lie. You must acknowledge your sin and confess it to the Lord.

B. Repentance is the other part of our response to sin. By repentance we turn from sin and begin to obey God. This is the subject of Lesson Six.

LESSON SIX: **HOW TO OVERCOME SIN—REPENTANCE**

Sin is a power to be conquered as well as a guilt to be forgiven. God not only forgives; He also changes us so that we will stop sinning. The power of sin resides in our sinful nature. As non-Christians we are bound over to the power of sin. In Jesus Christ the power of sin is broken. Our turning from sin to serve God is a lifelong process. The Bible calls this "repentance" (turning or changing) and "sanctification" (becoming holy).

I. Part One: *The Power of Sin*

A. Read John 8:34.

1. Who is a slave of sin? ____________________

2. Define the word "slave." ____________________

____

B. Read Ephesians 2:1-3.

1. What are you as a sinner? (v. 1) ____________________

2. What can a dead person do? ____________________

3. Whom did you follow?[1] ____________________

____

4. What did you gratify? ____________________

____

5. What were you by nature? ____________________

C. Read Romans 3:12.

1. What can a sinner not do? ____________________

____

---

1. The ruler of the kingdom of the air—Satan.

2. Do you think a sinner can change himself? ____________

3. What is the value of a sinner to God? ____________

D. Read I Corinthians 2:14.

1. What can a man without the Spirit not do? ____________

____

2. What are the things of the Spirit to non-Christians? ____________

____________ Why? ____________

____

3. Would such a person have any real interest in Christ? ____________

Sin is our master. As sinners we love sin and hate God. This is the condition of every man until he comes to Christ in faith. It is not that we are as bad as we could be, but that everything we do is imperfect and blighted by sin. In fact, we are so much under sin's control we have no power or desire to come to Christ for new life. We can outwardly reform our ways but we cannot change our hearts. This is what the Holy Spirit must do to bring us to Christ. (See Lesson Three, Part I, A.)

II. Part Two: *Christ's Victory over Sin*

A. Christ's Work for Us

1. Read John 8:34-36.

a. What can Christ alone do? ____________

b. Is there a middle ground between slavery and freedom? ____________

2. Read I Peter 2:24.

a. What did Christ do on the cross? ____________

____

b. What is the result? ____________

____

Christ alone can free us from sin's power. By His death he has put to death the power of sin. His work for us in history is the basis of the change in our personal lives. His death and resurrection are applied to our lives when we are joined to Christ by faith. We call this "union with Christ."

B. Our Union with Christ

1. Read Colossians 2:12.

   a. What has happened to you? ____________________

   ____

   b. How were you buried and raised with Christ?[2] ____________________

   ____

2. Read Romans 6:1-7.

   a. What is the purpose of our dying and rising with Christ? (vv. 4-7)

   ____

   ____

   b. What happened to our old sinful self? (v. 6) ____________________

   ____

   c. What is the outcome of the death of our old self? ____________________

   ____

   ____

3. Read Colossians 3:9-10.

   a. What have you taken off because of your union with Christ?

   ____

   b. What have you put on? ____________________

2. Baptism refers primarily to the Holy Spirit's uniting you to Jesus (I Corinthians 12:13). This is symbolized and sealed in water baptism.

The Spirit unites us to Christ by working faith in our hearts. The Holy Spirit being poured out on us, creating faith in us and binding us to Jesus is called "the baptism with the Holy Ghost." Water baptism (pouring water on a person) symbolizes this outpouring of the Spirit. Without the Holy Spirit we cannot become or continue to be Christians (I Corinthians 12:3, 13; Romans 8:9; I Corinthians 2:14; Ephesians 3:16-17). This is a great mystery. The Holy Spirit alone enables us to believe. Yet it is by faith that we receive Christ and His Spirit (Galatians 3:14). The Spirit unites us to Christ. Christ pours out the Spirit upon us (Acts 2:33). Again this union with Christ is a great mystery, for by this union we participate in the meaning and power of Christ's death and resurrection. He died for our sins. When we are united to Him, we die with Him. This means our old sinful nature is crucified and the enslaving power of sin is broken. Christ also rose for us; therefore we are raised with Him, our sins are forgiven and we are renewed. God begins to remake us into His image. Thus by dying and rising with Christ we are dead to sin's power and guilt, and alive to God. It is because of this mysterious union with Christ in His death and resurrection that we are able to stop sinning and begin obeying God. Christ died once for all. But when we are united to Him, we actually participate in the power of His death, and so we are said to die with Him. The same is true of His resurrection. We are united to Jesus as He is the crucified, raised, ascended and reigning Lord (Ephesians 2:6; Colossians 3:1-4). We are people of resurrection life because Christ shares His life with us.

III. Part Three: *How to Overcome Sin*

A. Our Attitude

1. Read Romans 6:11-13.

a. What should be your attitude toward sin? (v. 11) ________________

____

b. What should be your attitude toward God? ________________

____

c. What are you not to do? (vv. 12-13) ________________

____

____

d. What are you to do? (v. 13)______________________________

____

____

2. Read Colossians 3:5-8, 12-14.

   a. What are you to do to your earthly nature? (v. 5) ____________

   ____

   b. Do you see any of these qualities in you? ________________

   c. What are you to replace your evil habits with? ______________

   ____

We must count ourselves as dead to sin. We must put to death our sinful habits and desires. In their place we must put the qualities of love, patience, etc., and the actions and habits appropriate to Christians. So, for example, if we sometimes lie, we must stop and begin to tell the truth. Or if we steal, we must stop and begin to earn our own money. We put off or put to death the old ways and put on the new Christ-like ways.

B. Our Means and Power

1. The Holy Spirit: Read Romans 8:12-17.

   a. What must we not live according to? ____________________

   ____

   b. What must we do?______________________________

   ____

   c. Who supplies the power? ________________________

   d. What does it mean to be led by the Spirit? ______________

   ____

e. What will be the outcome of our sufferings in the struggle with sin? ____________________

The Spirit is the power by which we put to death sin and obey God. He makes Christ's death and resurrection a vital force in our lives. Perhaps you might take a few moments and review lesson three: How to Live by the Power of the Spirit. Pray and ask God the Spirit to help you.

2. The Word of God: Read John 8:31-32.

   a. What must you do to overcome sin? ____________________

   b. What must you know? ____________________

God's Word is our weapon in fighting sin. We cannot win without being immersed in the Word. The Spirit takes the Word and makes it effective in our lives. Regular Bible study with attention to how the Bible applies to us is indispensable to overcoming sin.

3. Faith (and Prayer): Read Galatians 2:20.

   a. Who is your true life? ____________________

   b. How do you live? ____________________

   ____

Faith is our depending on Christ to change us and renew us. Faith comes from the Holy Spirit working in the Word. Without faith we will surely fail for we will fill the void with our pride. Only by faith in Christ can we live the Christian life. Faith expresses itself in prayer. Because we believe God, we call out to Him.

4. Christians (Church Discipline): Read Galatians 6:1.

   a. What are you to do if you see a brother sin? ____________________

   ____

   b. What should be your attitude when you correct a brother?

   ____

c. If you are sinning, should you welcome the correction of other

Christians?______________________________________

The Christian life is not lived in isolation. You cannot overcome sin by yourself. You need others to correct and encourage you, and they need you.

So then, overcoming sin means living by faith in dependence on the Spirit, studying and applying God's Word to yourself and giving and receiving correction from other Christians. Your struggle with sin will last your entire earthly life. However, *by the Spirit's power* you *can* achieve progress and actually become more like Christ. The one sure road to failure is to try to overcome sin by your own strength. You must depend upon the power of the Spirit who unites you to Jesus. If you have a sinful habit you need to do the following: (1) Ask forgiveness and help from God. (2) Learn from God's Word how you should live. (3) Stop sinning. Break every connection with sin. Remove yourself physically from the source of temptation if possible. (4) Replace the old sinful habit with a new godly habit. For example, if you steal, stop stealing, get a job and give money to the needy. By the Holy Spirit's power put off the old way and put on the new way. Here is a chart to help you:

What my sin is	What God's Word says	Sinful actions and associations I must get rid of	Godly actions and associations I must put on

LESSON SEVEN: **HOW TO LOVE OTHERS**

As we learned in Lesson One, one of the ways we show our love and gratitude to God is by loving our neighbors. Our neighbor is anyone with whom we have contact. But, we also have a special relationship to other Christians that requires mutual love. We must not think that loving other people will be easy or painless. Loving is rather costly. God's love cost Him His only Son.

I. Part One: *Our Motive for Love*

A. God Is Love: Read I John 4:7-8

1. Why should we love? (v. 7) ______________________________

____

2. What is true about those who love? (v. 7) ____________________

____

3. Can you be a Christian if you do not love? (v. 8)______________

B. God Has Shown Us Love: Read I John 4:9-11.

1. How has God loved us? (vv. 9-10)__________________________

____

2. What should we do in response to God's love? (v. 11) __________

____

Our love for others comes from God's love for us. Apart from God's love, we cannot love others. It is only as we receive and acknowledge His love, that we are able to love. True love is contrary to our nature as sinners. Only God's love for us can change our wicked hearts into hearts full of love. It is as we come to understand more of Christ's love for us that we are able to increasingly love others. God is love, which for us means He is the source of love. Without Him we are not truly loved nor can we love others.

II. Part Two: *The Character of Love*

A. Love Is an Action: Read I John 3:16-18.

1. Who is the pattern for what love is? (v. 16) ______________________

2. What did Jesus do for us? (v. 16) ______________________

   ____

3. How should we respond to people in need? (v. 17) ______________________

   ____

   ____

4. Is it enough to talk about love? (v. 18) ______________________

5. How are we to love? (v. 18) ______________________

   ____

6. Can you think of someone to show love to this week? ______________________

   ____

7. Make a list of some specific things to do for others. ______________________

   ____

   ____

   ____

   ____

B. Love Is an Attitude: Read I Corinthians 13:4-8.

1. List the positive characteristics of love. ______________________

   ____

   ____

   ____

   ____

2. List what love is not. ______________________________

____

____

____

____

3. Whom do you know who has such a love for you? ______________

Love is an attitude and a pattern of action. When I love someone I consider his or her welfare above my own (Philippians 2:3) and I take action to secure his or her best interests (Philippians 2:4). Love is not a feeling. God commands me to love even my enemies toward whom I can hardly be expected to feel "warmth." God's love is the pattern for our love. God's Word is the rule that guides us to understand what love is. Unfortunately, much of our culture uses the term "love" for what in actuality is "selfish lust." Only God's law enables us to see true love and distinguish it from "lust." Indeed, love is the fulfillment of the law (Galatians 5:14; Romans 13:9-10). To love God is to keep His commandments (I John 5:3). To love men is to think and act toward them as God commands us to think and act (I John 5:2).

III. Part Three: *The People We Love*

A. Loving Other Christians (The Church)

1. What the Church Is

a. Read Romans 12:4-5.

(1) What are Christians? ______________________________

____

(2) What is our relationship to each other? ______________

____

(3) What would happen if the parts of a body began to fight with each other? ______________________________

____

b. Read Ephesians 1:19-23.

(1) What is under Christ's authority? (vv. 21-22) ____________

____

(2) What is the church? (v. 23) ______________________

____

c. Read Ephesians 2:19-22.

(1) What are you as a Christian? (v. 19) _______________

____

____

(2) List four different descriptions of what the church is? (vv. 19, 21, 22)

1. ____

2. ____

3. ____

4. ____

(3) What is the foundation of the church? (v. 20) ____________

____

The church is the body of Christ, the people of God. It includes every true believer in every age. Only God knows the exact number of those who are and will be His (II Timothy 2:19). Hence we speak of the "invisible church," meaning the whole company of God's elect people. However, the church also manifests itself in this world. This is called the "visible church." It is made up of all who profess Christ and their children. The visible church is divided into many local congregations of believers which are ruled (guided in love) by elders or pastors. You should belong to such a local body of believers. It is in the context of the local church that you can love and be loved by other Christians. It is the fellowship of those who share in Christ. Remember, the local church has many in it who may only pretend to be Christians. These are weeds among the wheat (Matthew 13:24-32).

2. Leadership in the Church

a. Read Ephesians 4:11-13.

(1) Whom has Christ given to help His people? (v. 11)

____

____

(2) Which are still in existence today?[1] ______________________________

____

(3) What are pastors and teachers to do? (v. 12) ______________

____

(4) What is their goal? (vv. 12-13)______________________

____

b. Read Hebrews 13:17.

(1) What should be your attitude to your Christian pastors or elders? ______________________________

(2) Why should you obey them? ______________________

____

God has ordained that there should be certain leaders in His church. These are variously called pastors, elders, or overseers (bishops). They refer to the same office. Their task is to preach, teach, encourage and rebuke God's people. You need them for your own spiritual growth. It is part of your love to other Christians that you respect and obey your leaders (provided what they say accords with Scripture). They are to love you even if that means rebuking you when you sin.

3. Life in the Church: Read Colossians 3:12-17.

---

1. Apostles and prophets were only for the founding of the church. There are no apostles or prophets today (Ephesians 2:19-20). However, their work is preserved in the documents of the New Testament.

a. With what are God's people to clothe themselves? (v. 12)

____

____

____

____

b. What should we do when Christians sin against us? (v. 13)

____

____

Why?______________________________________

c. What does love do? (v. 14) ______________________________________

____

d. What should dwell in us and rule in our hearts? (vv. 15-16)[2]

____

e. What should be the result? (vv. 16-17)______________________________________

____

The life of the church is a life of love. Love means forgiveness and patience towards others. We are to live at peace with one another. We are to care for each other and we are to corporately worship our God. As a member of a local congregation you need to seek ways to love and serve others. You need to be willing to forgive their faults. The relations of Christians should be governed by love at all times. In this way we all grow to be more like Jesus who loved us and gave Himself for us.

B. Loving Non-Christians

1. Non-Christians in General: Read Galatians 6:10.

a. To whom should we do good?______________________________________

2. The peace of Christ is the reconciliation with God which Christ accomplished in His death. The Word of Christ is that message of reconciliation—the gospel.

b. Should you love only Christians? ______________________

c. Can you think of a non-Christian for whom you could do something good? ______________________

2. Those Who Hate Us: Read Luke 6:27-28, 36.

a. What should be your attitude toward enemies? (v. 27) __________

____

____

b. What should you do to people who hurt you? (v. 28) __________

____

c. Why should you be merciful? (v. 36) ______________________

____

____

God wants us to love our enemies the way He loved us when we were His enemies (Romans 5:8). This is not easy, but God does not expect us to love in our own strength. It is our love for enemies that shows the true character of Christian love. In this way we imitate our Lord who loved us while we were still His enemies. Loving non-Christians is part of being a witness for Christ. Perhaps you were brought to Christ through the love and concern of a Christian.[3]

IV. Part Four: *How to Love*

Love is not something we can do in our own power. We need God to help us love others.

A. Knowing God's Love

1. Read I John 4:19-20.

a. Why can we love? ______________________

---

3. Loving enemies, however, does not mean you should not defend yourself or others if you or they are physically attacked. You have a duty to protect your life and the lives of others from lawless assaults (Exodus 22:2; Psalm 82:3-4; 118:10-11; 140; 144:1-2).

b. Can you love God and not your neighbor? ____________

c. What are you if you say "I love God" but do not love others?____

2. Read Romans 5:5.

a. What has God poured out in our hearts? ____________

b. By whom has He done this? ____________

3. Read Colossians 3:13.

a. What are you to do?____________

b. Why are you to do it? ____________

4. Read John 15:9-12.

a. Who has loved us? (v. 9)____________

b. What are we to do? (v. 9) ____________

c. How? (v. 10)____________

d. What does Jesus command us to do? (v. 12)____________

On our own, we will not be able to love. We must always look back to Jesus who loved us. As we accept and reflect on God's love for us we will be able to love others. We must learn to say to ourselves: "I will love this person because God loves me." The more we are grasped by God's love, the more we will love. You should daily contemplate God's love for you and seek to love others out of gratitude to God for His love.

B. Trusting God to Help

Just as you must receive God's love in order to love, you must depend upon God to help you love. Ask Him to help you to love others and trust that He will. In others words, love by faith.

1. Read Philippians 4:13.

   a. What could Paul do through Christ? ____________________

   b. What was Paul's attitude? ____________________

2. Read Philippians 4:6.

   a. What are you to pray for? ____________________

   b. Should you ask for help in loving others? ____________________

So then, to love others you need to do three things: First, you must accept and meditate on God's love for you. Second, you must ask God to help you and depend on Him. Third, take action! Begin loving! Look for specific needs and meet them. Plan something to do for someone else. Visit a sick person. Help someone with chores. *Do it!* Use the following chart as an aid to begin loving others in deed and not just word.

People I Could Help	How I Could Help Them	When I Will Do It

LESSON EIGHT: **HOW TO ENDURE SUFFERING**

Christians cannot escape suffering of one kind or another. Indeed, no man living in this evil age will be free from pain, whether it is the torment of physical pain or the torture of emotional hurt. However, Christians are at peace with God. Why should we suffer? The Bible gives us a number of reasons for suffering. To a large extent the quality of your Christian life will only appear in the presence of adversity.

I. Part One: *Suffering and Our Sin*

A. Suffering as Discipline for Our Sin: Read Hebrews 12:1-11.

1. What will God do to His sons? (vv. 5-6) ____________________

____

2. How should we regard hardship? (v. 7) ____________________

____

3. What should be our attitude when God disciplines us for our sin? (v. 9)____________________

4. Why does God discipline us? (v. 10) ____________________

____

5. What is the result of His discipline? (v. 11) ____________________

____

6. What must you do if you are to endure hardship? (vv. 2-3) ____________________

____

7. What will happen if you do not consider Jesus? (v. 3) ____________________

____

Christians may suffer because they sin. Such suffering is not a legal punishment and a foretaste of the pains of hell as it is for unbelievers. Rather hardship comes as God's discipline to cure us from our sins, that is, that we might partake of His holiness. We must not blame God but rather submit to His discipline and learn to stop sinning. This will only happen as we focus upon Jesus. Because He suffered for us, our sufferings serve not as a foreshadowing of God's eternal wrath, but as a means of making us holy, for our own good.

B. Suffering as a Result of Our Struggle with Sin

1. Read Romans 7:21-25

 a. Describe Paul's problem? (vv. 21-23) ____________________

 ____

 ____

 b. How does Paul characterize himself? (v. 24) ______________

 ____

 c. Have you ever experienced this?______________________

 Our struggle with sin means real suffering. There is the grief of knowing we offend our God. There is also the painful longing to be free from sin completely. This is an inner but a very powerful form of suffering.

2. Read Romans 8:12-23.

 a. What is our obligation? (vv. 12-13) ____________________

 ____

 ____

 b. What does the Spirit lead us to do? (vv. 13-14)______________

 ____

 c. If the Spirit so leads what is our assurance? (vv. 14-16)________

 ____

 ____

d. In this struggle with sin, whose sufferings do we share? (v. 17)

____

e. What was the outcome of His sufferings? ______________

f. What will be the outcome of ours? ______________

g. What should our estimate of our sufferings be? (v. 18) ________

____

h. What should we hope for? (v. 23)[1] ______________

By the Spirit we struggle with sin. The Spirit leads us into the battle and the suffering. We must not lose heart. Our suffering in overcoming sin is a sharing of Christ's sufferings and so assures us of a share in His glory. The pattern of His life, suffering then glory, must be duplicated in us. This is why we long for His return, for that will be our entrance into glory and our final victory over sin in the resurrection of our bodies.

II. Part Two: *Suffering and Our Faith*

A. Read James 1:2-4.

1. What should be your attitude when you face trials? (v. 2) ________

____

2. What is the purpose of your trials? (v. 3) ______________

____

3. What is the outcome of this testing? (v. 3) ______________

____

4. Where does perseverance lead? (v. 4) ______________

____

B. Read Romans 5:3-5.

---

1. The redemption of our bodies is a reference to resurrection at Christ's return.

1. What are the qualities that suffering produces? (vv. 3-4)__________

____

____

2. Why does hope not disappoint? (v. 5) ____________________

____

____

C. Read I Peter 1:6-7.

1. In what should you rejoice? ____________________

____

2. What do trials prove about your faith? ____________________

____

3. What will be the result of a proven faith? ____________________

______________ When? ____________________

Suffering often occurs not because of our sin. God sends difficulties to mature us so that our faith may be proven and its fruit produced. Suffering produces in our personality the qualities of Jesus. It teaches us to persevere, to mature and to hope in God. We should greet such trials with joy because we know God is using them to make us like Jesus.

III. Part Three: *Suffering for Christ and Righteousness*

A. Suffering for Doing Good (Righteousness)

1. Read I Peter 2:18-25.

a. Whom should you consider when you suffer for doing what is right? (v. 19) ____________________

____

b. What is God's attitude when you suffer unjustly? __________

____

c. Are such sufferings to surprise you?__________ Why? (v. 21)

____

d. Who is your example in suffering? (v. 21) ________________

e. What was Christ's response to suffering? (v. 23) ____________

____

____

2. Read I Peter 3:13-17.

a. What are you when you suffer for doing good? (v. 14)________

____

b. Should you be afraid? ______________________________

c. What should you do? (v. 15)__________________________

____

____

____

d. How should you testify for Christ? (v. 16) ________________

____

e. What will be the result?______________________________

____

Suffering for doing good is a blessing because Christ also suffered as the righteous for the unrighteous. Suffering for the good we do means following in Christ's steps. Rather than fearing such trials we should enthrone Christ as Lord in our hearts and seek to bear witness of Him. In this we can endure the suffering and bring glory to God. Even our adversaries will be ashamed at their accusation when we live godly lives before them.

B. Suffering for the Name of Christ: Read I Peter 4:12-19.

1. When you suffer for Christ in whose sufferings do you participate?

(v. 13)____

2. What should be your attitude? (v. 13) ______________________

____

3. To what should you look forward? (v. 13)____________________

____

4. Why are you blessed? (v. 14)____________________________

____

5. For what should you *not* suffer? (v. 15)____________________

____

____

6. What should be your response to suffering? (v. 16)___________

____

(v. 19)____

When we suffer for Christ we participate in Christ's sufferings. So we will also partake of His glory. We must commit ourselves to God and continue to do good. To suffer for Christ is a privilege for which we ought to praise God. Remember, suffering now means glory later.

So then, suffering is always for our good. Some suffering is God's discipline to cure us from sin. Other suffering is the result of our inner struggle with sin. Sometimes suffering is a test of our faith. Even for doing good and being faithful to Christ we may suffer. Let us not revile God but bless Him for our pain. In suffering we are being conformed to Christ who suffered for us so that we may be glorified with Him when He comes again on that last day. Let us acknowledge Christ as our Lord and bear patiently our present trial which is not worthy of comparison with the glory that is to be ours with Christ. Suffering is one way God purifies His people. True believers are enabled by the Holy Spirit to endure and to rejoice in God. Hypocrites will turn their praise to blasphemy when suffering comes. Suffering is part of the character of being a Christian. Someone who paints the Christian life as just joy and happiness knows little of Scripture. The glory of the Christian life is that in the midst of trial we are able to rejoice in our God. Even in sadness we rejoice, for our God will one day bring us into His presence forever.

LESSON NINE: **HOW TO DEAL WITH YOUR EMOTIONS**

In this lesson we will consider four very troublesome emotions: fear, worry, anger or bitterness, and depression. All of us have experienced all of these at some time in our lives. In fact, you may be dominated by one of these to such an extent that it spoils your fellowship with God and hinders your obedience to him. God's Word has some very definite things to say about fear, worry, anger or bitterness, and depression. When we discuss these we should be clear that we are not concerned with mere feelings, such as the feelings of fear one has when he is about to fall, but with attitudes and patterns of actions that we call fear, worry, anger or bitterness, and depression. I cannot help *feeling* afraid of large dogs. I can refuse to *think* and *act* fearfully around large dogs. We cannot control how we feel. We can control (by God's power) how we think and act.

I. Part One: *Fear and Worry*

A. Proper and Improper Fear

1. Read Ecclesiastes 12:13.

a. What two things are we to do as our duty? ____________________

____

b. Is all fear wrong then?____________________

c. What kind of fear is proper? ____________________

2. Read Matthew 10:27-31.

a. What kind of fear is improper? (v. 28) ____________________

____

b. Why? (vv. 29-31) ____________________

____

c. Whom should you fear? ____________________

3. Read I Peter 3:13-14.

   a. What are you not to fear?[1] ______________________________

   ____

   b. List some things that frighten non-Christians. ______________

   ____

   ____

   ____

We are to fear God. However, we are forbidden to fear men, their opinions or actions, and to fear the things men fear—death, sickness, poverty, etc. The fears of non-Christians immobilize them so they cannot act properly as God commands. The fear of God frees us from human fears so we will do God's will. The fear of God is the reverence and awe we have toward Him who is eternal, unchangeable and sovereign, while we are needy, weak, and dependent. There is also a bodily reaction that is called fear. This is the physiological state in which adrenalin is released, muscles tense, and the body prepares for action. This is God's built-in protection device. This kind of "fear" is good and not condemned by the Bible. The feeling of danger when standing on a cliff keeps us from falling. Perhaps we should not call this "fear." The fear the Bible forbids is a fearful attitude that keeps us from obeying God. Actually improper fear is just unbelief.

B. Wrong and Legitimate Concern

1. Read Matthew 6:25-34.

   a. List the things that you should not worry about? (vv. 25, 31, 34) _

   ____

   ____

   ____

   b. Is there anything left to worry about? ______________________

2. Read James 4:13-17.

---

1. They = non-Christians.

a. Is there a wrong way to plan for the future? ______________

b. Is there a proper way? ______________

c. What is the proper way? ______________

____

____

Worry is our attempt to control the future. It immobilizes us because it shifts our attention from the present and the duties of the present. "Anyone who knows the good he ought to do and doesn't do it, sins." Worry, like fear, keeps us from serving God. However, there is a proper way to plan for the future, that is, to do something now (make plans) that will affect the future. Such plans, however, must always recognize that it is God who rules the future, and so our plans may not be accomplished.

C. God's Solution to Improper Fear and to Worry

1. God's Sovereignty: Read Ephesians 1:11.

   a. Does God have a plan for all history? ______________

   b. How much does God work out in conformity to His purpose? ______________

   ____

   c. Do things happen by chance or fate? ______________

   d. Is God in absolute control of your life? ______________

2. God's Promise: Read Romans 8:28.

   a. What does God do for those who love Him? ______________

   ____

   b. Do even the painful parts of life have an ultimately good purpose and result? ______________

   c. Is there anything in life to fear? ______________

3. Read Romans 8:38-39.

   a. Can you be separated from Christ? ______________

b. What created thing should you fear?____________________

4. Reread Matthew 6:32-33.

a. Does God promise to provide all your needs?________________

b. What is there left to worry about?____________________

God is the absolute Lord of all history who causes everything to happen just as He planned. This is why fear and worry are improper (except the fear of God). Fear and worry are sin because they are practical denials of both God's love and His power. When we are controlled by fear or worry, we are saying to God, "You don't have the power to help" or "You don't love me enough to help." Those are lies!

D. Overcoming Habits of Fear and Worry

1. Focusing upon God's Promises (Faith)

a. Read I Peter 3:13-15.

(1) What are you to do instead of fear? (v. 15) ____________

____

(2) What does this mean?________________________

____

b. Read Psalm 37:1-5.

(1) What should you do instead of fretting (worrying)?

____

____

____

____

____

(2) What will the Lord do?_______________________

____

____

2. Calling upon God (Prayer): Read Philippians 4:4-7.

   a. What should you pray about? (v. 6) ____________________

   b. What should you do besides ask? (v. 6) ____________________

   ____

   c. What does God promise? (v. 7)____________________

   ____

   d. Should you rejoice? (v. 4)__________Why?__________

   ____

3. Obeying God First

   a. Read Matthew 6:31-34 again.

      (1) What are you to do instead of worrying? ____________

      ____

      (2) What does it mean to seek first God's kingdom?__________

      ____

      ____

      ____

      ____

   b. Read Ecclesiastes 12:13 again.

      (1) What should you do instead of fearing men? __________

      ____

      (2) Is your fear an excuse for not keeping God's commandments?

      ____

The solution to fear and worry is simple. We must focus on God's promises, call out to God for help confessing our sin and praising Him, and then get on with the business of obeying God. It is impossible to fear and worry while you praise God and rejoice in Him. We must obey God first regardless of whether we feel afraid. Our love and fear of God will lead us to obey Him. "Mature love casts out fear" (John 4:18).

II. Part Two: *Anger and Bitterness*

A. Anger and Bitterness Are Forbidden: Read Ephesians 4:30-32.

1. What are you to get rid of? (v. 31) ______________________

____

2. Whom do you grieve when you exhibit the above qualities? (v. 30)

____

3. What should you put in place of anger and bitterness? (v. 32)

____

Anger (lashing out at people or things) and bitterness (boiling inside about people or things) are out of place in the Christian. They are the opposite of the love and forgiveness we are to have. They poison us and hurt others. Most importantly, they grieve God the Spirit.

B. How to Deal with Anger and Bitterness

1. Following the Example of Christ: Read I Peter 2:21-23.

a. Did Christ react in bitterness or anger? ______________

b. How did He react? ______________________________

____

c. How should you react to unjust punishment? ____________

____

d. Do you have a right to be angry or bitter even if you're not at fault?

____

2. Some Practical Suggestions: Read Ephesians 4:26-32.

a. When you feel angered,[2] should you go to bed that way? (v. 26)________Why? (v. 27)________________________

b. When someone angers you, how should you talk with him? (v. 29)

____

____

c. What should your words do?________________________

____

d. Should you grant forgiveness if wronged? (v. 32) ____________

e. Why?________________________________

____

Do not let anger or bitterness fester. Deal with it immediately. Begin by granting forgiveness because Christ has forgiven you. Then deal constructively with the problem rather than attacking people with your words. Anger as a motivating emotion helps you get problems solved. However, anger as lashing out at people (or things) is sin. When the emotion of anger is misused, as in lashing out, we call that sinful anger. When the emotion is held in and festers, we call it bitterness. Feeling angry is not sin; thinking and acting angrily or bitterly is sin.

III. Part Three: *Depression*

A. What Depression Is

Depression is that state in which we are discouraged and have given up hope. When we are depressed we think about our problems or sins and continue to do nothing about them. We just sit and sulk. Depression keeps us from doing what we are supposed to do. Since we do not do what we should (because we are depressed) our problem gets worse and we become more depressed. Soon we are completely immobilized.

B. God's Solution to Depression

1. Changing Our Focus: Read Philippians 4:4-9.

2. Remember, it is anger as lashing out at people that is sin. The feeling of anger (displeasure) is not sin. (There is also a proper holy anger, e.g., God's anger at sinners.)

a. In whom should we rejoice? (v. 4) ______________________

b. When? ____

c. What should we occupy our minds with? (v. 8) ____________

____

d. Should this lead us to action? (v. 9) ___________________

2. Changing Our Actions: Read Genesis 4:2-7.

a. Why did Cain become downcast? (vv. 3-5) _______________

____

____

b. What did God tell Cain to do? (v. 7) ___________________

____

____

c. What would have happened had he done what was right? _____

____

d. What did God warn Cain about? _______________________

____

____

The solution to depression is a change in thoughts and in actions. We must shift our focus from ourselves to Christ and rejoice in Him. Likewise, we must stop doing nothing and begin to obey God by doing what He says is right. As you change your thoughts to focus on Christ and your actions to obey Christ, the feeling of depression will pass. But you must take action now. God requires it!

LESSON TEN: **HOW TO HAVE A CHRISTIAN MARRIAGE**

The most basic of all human relationships is that between a husband and a wife. All other relationships, except your relationship to God, take second place to this relationship. God Himself ordained marriage for the good of the man at the creation. Yet sin has twisted, distorted and corrupted this good gift of God. Therefore, Christians must be instructed from the Bible about how they are to live as husbands and wives.

I. Part One: *The Marriage Bond*

A. God's Plan for Marriage: Read Genesis 2:18-25.

1. What did God decide was not good for man? (v. 18) ________________

____

2. What did God decide to do for man? (v. 18) ________________

____

____

3. What could not be found for man among the animals? (vv. 19-20) ____

____

4. How did God make a suitable helper for man? (vv. 21-22) __________

____

____

____

5. What was man's reaction to God's gift of the woman? (v. 23) ______

____

6. Whom does a man leave when he is united to his wife? (v. 24) ______

____

7. What do man and woman become in marriage? (v. 24) ______________

____

God gave marriage to man for it was not good to be alone. From this we learn the basic function of marriage is companionship. It is the most intimate of companionships, for the two become one flesh. In other words, they share all their lives, their possessions and their goals. They live and act not as two but as one. This intimacy, expressed in the sex act, is only to be shared by one woman and one man. So basic is this relationship that man in marriage ceases to be under the authority of his father and becomes the authority in a new family.

B. God's Requirement of Fidelity: Read Matthew 19:4-6.

1. Who joins together a man and a woman? ______________________

2. What must man not do? ______________________________

____

3. Is divorce part of God's plan for marriage? ____________________

The marriage bond is a life-long bond. It bonds one man and one woman together until one dies. So then, one ought not to enter marriage flippantly. Likewise, problems in a marriage are not an excuse for divorce but a summons to work harder to solve those problems. To destroy a marriage by an unwarranted divorce (either legally through the courts or practically by desertion) brings one under the condemnation of God.

C. Divorce and Remarriage

1. Read Matthew 19:8-9.

a. What does a person commit when he divorces and remarries? (v. 9)

____

b. What is the grounds for divorce that allows the remarriage of the innocent party without sin? ______________________

2. Read I Corinthians 7:12-15.

a. May a believer divorce his or her spouse because the spouse is *not* a believer? (vv. 12-13). ______

b. What should a believer do if the unbelieving spouse deserts him or her? (v. 15) ______

______

c. If the believer has been faithful may he or she remarry? (i.e., is he or she free?) (v. 15) ______

God did not ordain divorce in the beginning. However, because of man's sin, God graciously allows the innocent party to break the marriage bond by divorce without incurring sin. The only two reasons for this are adultery on the part of the spouse or desertion by an unbeliever of a believer. In no other instance does a person have the right of divorce. All other divorce *is sin*. Even in such situations as adultery or desertion by an unbeliever, the innocent spouse is not required to seek a divorce. Divorce, it should be remembered, is not part of God's original plan for marriage.

II. Part Two: *The Roles of Husbands and Wives*

A. Wives: Read Ephesians 5:22-24.

1. Describe the wife's role. (vv. 22-24) ______

______

2. When the wife submits to the husband, to whom else does she submit? (v. 22) ______

3. What is the parallel between husbands and wives and between Christ and the church? (v. 23) ______

______

B. Husbands: Read Ephesians 5:25-33.

1. Describe the husband's role. (v. 25) ______

______

2. How is a husband to love his wife? (v. 25)________________

____

3. What did Christ do because He loved the church? (vv. 25-27)

____

4. What should a husband do in loving his wife?________________

____

5. Should a husband have more concern for himself than for his wife? (vv. 28, 33) ________________

In marriage the husband is to love his wife. He is her head, yet he bears authority not to "lord it over" her but to help, and encourage her. He is to be willing to sacrifice himself and his desires for the good of his wife. The wife is to submit to her husband (unless he tells her to do something that violates God's law). This is not the submission of a slave but the loving submission of an equal heir of eternal life in order to please Christ and benefit her husband. Two heads in one marriage means trouble. God has placed the man as the head, but has done so for the good of the woman. He is to love her sacrificially and she is to submit to and respect him because she submits to Christ.

III. Part Three: *Solving Problems in Marriage*

A. Seeking Forgiveness: Read Matthew 7:1-5.

1. What are you not to do? (v. 1) ________________

2. Whose sin must you deal with first, yours or your spouse's? (vv. 3-5)

____

When a problem arises, first examine your own life. Before you dare confront your spouse with his or her sin, confess your own sin to your spouse and ask to be forgiven.

B. Granting Forgiveness: Read Ephesians 4:31-32.

1. Do you have the right to be angry and bitter when your spouse does something to hurt you? (v. 31)________________

2. What should you do? (v. 32) ______________________

____

Why? ______________________

____

When an argument flares up, first confess your sin; then if your spouse has hurt you, forgive him or her. Restore your relationship by mutual forgiveness. Paul warns that we should not let the sun go down on our anger (Ephesians 4:26-27). Seek forgiveness and grant it. Then you are ready to tackle the problem.

C. Attacking Problems Not People

1. Read Ephesians 4:29.

a. What is not supposed to come out of your mouth? ______________________

____

b. What should your words do? ______________________

2. Read James 1:19.

a. What should you be quick to do? ______________________

b. What should you be slow to do? ______________________

Solve problems by attacking problems, not your spouse. Your conversations should be directed to building up, not tearing down, your spouse. Direct your efforts and energy at the problem "according to their needs." Here is a simple 3-step plan for solving difficulties: (1) confess your sin to your spouse; (2) grant forgiveness if needed to your spouse; (3) together attack the problem, not each other. These principles can be applied to other relationships also. If you are struggling with problems in your marriage, do not try to solve them alone. Ask for the help of your pastor or elder. He can help you apply these principles to the specific needs of the situation.

A helpful way to apply these principles is the "conference table" technique. See Appendix to Lesson Ten, "Setting Up a Conference Table."

LESSON ELEVEN: **HOW TO USE YOUR RESOURCES**

Jesus is the Lord. This most basic of Christian confessions has implications for every aspect of life. Jesus demands that our allegiance to Him be demonstrated in our thoughts and in our relationships with others. But Jesus also is Lord of our resources of time, money and property. As a Christian, how you use your resources is not a matter of merely personal taste. God has a plan for your life that includes even your stewardship of your resources.

I. Part One: *Perspectives on Your Resources*

A. God Is the Owner of All Things.

1. Read Psalm 24:1-2.

a. Who owns the earth and what it contains? ____________________

b. Who owns the inhabitants of the earth? ____________________

c. Who owns your most favored possession? ____________________

d. Why is God the owner of all things?____________________

____

2. Read James 1:17.

a. Where does every good gift come from?____________________

____

b. Whom should you thank for your money and possessions? ______

______________Why?______________________________

____

B. God Is the Ruler of All Things.

1. Read Job 14:5.

a. Is the length of man's life determined? ______________________

____

b. By whom is it determined? ______________________

c. Is your time your own? ______________________

2. Read Isaiah 45:7.

a. Who brings prosperity into your life? ______________________

____

b. Does disaster come as the result of some chance event unplanned by God? ______________________

c. Is your physical well-being a matter of happenstance? ______________

____

d. Who, then, rules your time and your resources? ______________

____

The Bible's view of things is much different from sinful man's opinions. Religion is no private matter, for Jesus is Lord of all. The Christian who says, "My money is my own; I'll do with it as I please" has not yet understood the very basics of the faith. Our God rules all. All we have are His gifts. Even the span of our lives is determined by His eternal plan. Even with our resources, God is always Lord and we are always servants.

II. Part Two: *How to Use Your Time and Energy*

A. Good Stewardship of Time and Energy

1. Read Ephesians 5:15-16.

a. How are you to live? (v. 15) ______________________

b. Should you waste time? (v. 16) ______________________

c. What should you do? (v. 16) ______________________

____

d. Why? (v. 16)______________________________

2. Read II Thessalonians 3:10-12.

a. Is idleness pleasing to God? (v. 11) ______________________

b. What do idle people often become? (v. 11) ________________

____

c. What are we to do instead of being idle? (vv. 10, 12)__________

____

B. Priorities in Your Use of Time and Energy

1. Time with God

a. Read Psalms 119:9-11.

(1) How can you keep your way pure? (v. 9)______________

____

(2) What must you spend time doing? (v. 11) ____________

____

b. Read Colossians 4:2-4.

(1) What should you devote yourself to?______________

(2) What should you pray about?____________________

____

2. Time Working: Read I Thessalonians 4:11-12

a. What are you to be ambitious about? (Three things)

(1) ______________________________

(2) ______________________________

(3) ______________________________

b. Why should you do these thing: (Two Reasons)

(1) ______________________________

(2) ______________________________

3. Time with Family: Read Ephesians 5:22-6:4.

   a. What are wives to do? (vv. 22, 33) ____________________

   ____

   b. What are husbands to do? (vv. 25, 33) ____________________

   ____

   c. What are parents to do? (6:4) ____________________

   ____

   d. What are children to do? (6:1-3) ____________________

   ____

4. Time with the Body of Christ: Read Hebrews 10:25.

   a. What are we not to give up? ____________________

   ____

   b. What are we to do? ____________________

   ____

   c. Is fellowship and worship with other Christians an option? ______

5. Time in Service to Others

   a. Read Galatians 6:10.

      (1) To whom should we do good? ____________________

      (2) When or how often? ____________________

      ____

   b. Read James 1:27.

      (1) Should we care only for ourselves? ____________________

      (2) Whom else should we look after?[1] ____________________

   c. Read Colossians 4:5-6.

1. Widows and orphans include also the poor and sick who are downtrodden and helpless.

(1) Should we look for opportunities to witness?______________

(2) Do you regularly witness? ______________________________

Times with God, in labor, with family, with the church and in helping others are all required. We need to schedule our time so that we accomplish these things first. Then we may take time for recreation, hobbies and just sitting around. We must take care to use our time wisely. We have certain obligations that cannot be put aside. We must spend time alone with God in prayer and Bible study. We must work. We must spend time with family, in church, and ministering to others. Everything else takes second place. Also we must not spend so much time at work that we have no time for family or church. You must schedule your time so you can meet all of your responsibilities. No one thing can use up all your time, not even Bible study and prayer. Our time must be carefully apportioned according to God's Word. In planning your time, God requires you to rest from your normal labors one day out of seven. This weekly day of rest is called the Sabbath (Exodus 20:8-11). Ask your pastor for advice about how to observe the Sabbath. At the end of this lesson is an exercise to help you evaluate how you can use your time and energy.

III. Part Three: *How to Use Your Money and Possessions*

A. The Needs of Your Family

1. Read I Timothy 5:8.

a. Whom should you provide for?______________________________

____

b. What are you if you do not? ______________________________

____

2. Read Titus 3:14.

a. What should you do?______________________________

____

b. Why? (two reasons) ______________________________

____

B. The Elders (Ministers, Pastors) Who Instruct You

1. Read I Timothy 5:17-18.

   a. Who is worthy of double honor?

   b. Does he deserve his wage?

2. Read Galatians 6:6.

   a. What should you share with ministers?

   b. Do you contribute regularly to the salary of your minister or pastor?

C. Those in Need

1. Read I Timothy 6:17-18.

   a. What should a well-to-do person not do? (v. 17)

   b. What should he do? (vv. 17-18) (four things)

   c. Should you be selfish with your wealth?

2. Read II Corinthians 9:6-9.

   a. Does God want you to give reluctantly? (v. 7)

   b. Who must decide how much you will give to help others? (v. 7)

c. If you give, will God leave you out on a limb, so to speak? (vv. 6, 9) ____________

You have a serious responsibility for how you use your money and possessions. You need to provide for your family's daily needs (if you are in a position to do so). If you are still a child, then that obviously is not yet your job. You also need to give to support your minister who preaches the Word of God to you. But you are also responsible to give to others in need. This may mean helping a poor family pay for food or giving to support a foreign missionary. Your money is not yours to use as you please but is a trust from God to use according to His Word. God, who owns all that you have and are, requires that you return to Him 10 percent of your income or earnings. This is called the tithe and it is to be used for the ministry of the church, for spreading the gospel, and for the care of the poor (Deuteronomy 14:22, 28-29). On top of this tithe you may give more as you see others in need and as you have plenty (I Timothy 6:17-19). Your pastor or elder can advise you in this matter.

One way to use money carefully is to have a budget so that you plan thoughtfully where your money goes. It will also help you not to get into debt and need someone else to bail you out. There is an exercise at the end of the study to help you budget your money.

TIME

List your activities for this week. (How did you use your time?)	List your responsibilities according to the Bible.
work personal worship church	provide for my family help others

1. Circle those responsibilities you did not adequately do.
2. Circle those activities that are not necessary and could be eliminated.

3. Now make out a schedule for next week taking the time that was wasted and using it for those responsibilities you did not fulfill.(If you are largely not fulfilling your responsibilities, you might want to ask your pastor for advice.)

MONEY

1. On what did you waste money?
2. If you had not wasted money, how much would you have to give to others? (Remember, it is not wrong to spend money on yourself. It is wrong to spend money only for yourself when others have pressing needs.)
3. Fill in the following as an aid to learn how to budget your money.

Income: (per month)____________________________(net, not gross)
Expenses:

Housing (Rent or Mortgage)	__________
Utilities (gas, water, etc.)	__________
Phone	__________
Food	__________
Car Payments	__________
Car Repairs, Gasoline	__________
Clothing, Household Items	__________
Money for the church	__________
Gifts to the Needy (diaconal fund)	__________
Entertainment	__________
Other	__________

TOTAL EXPENDITURE FOR MONTH ________________

LESSON TWELVE: **HOW TO WITNESS TO OTHERS**

As Christians we are called to be witnesses for Jesus. We all have the responsibility of presenting the Good News about Jesus to others. Certainly there are Christians who work full-time in sharing the gospel, but this does not relieve us of the duty to also witness for Christ to the people we have contact with. Peter writes, "But you are a chosen people, a royal priesthood, a holy nation, a people belonging to God, that you may declare the praises of Him who called you out of darkness into His wonderful light."

I. Part One: *The Motivation to Witness—God's Command*

A. Our Corporate Responsibility as God's People

1. The Command of Christ: Read Matthew 28:18-20.

a. What does Jesus have? (v. 18) ____________________

b. What are we to do? (v. 19) ____________________

____

c. What are we to teach? (v. 20) ____________________

____

2. An Example from History: Read I Thessalonians 1:4-10.

a. How did the gospel come to the Thessalonians? (v. 5) __________

____

____

b. How did they welcome the message? (v. 6) ____________________

____

c. What was the result? (v. 8) ____________________

____

B. The Power to Witness (The Holy Spirit).

1. God's Promise to the Church: Read Acts 1:8.[1]

a. What does Jesus promise?____________________

b. What will Christians be?____________________

c. Where? ____________________

____

2. An Example from History: Read Acts 4:23-31.

a. What did the Christians pray for? (vv. 29-30)____________________

____

b. What was God's response? (v. 31) ____________________

____

c. What did the Christians do when they were filled with the Spirit?

____

Jesus has commanded us to be His witnesses. That is our motivation. Our commission comes directly from the King of kings. Christ also gives us His Spirit to empower us for the task. We ought to call out to God to fill us with the Spirit that we might faithfully witness for Christ. So then, we can be witnesses for Jesus because He commands us and because He empowers us by the Spirit. We simply have no valid excuse for not witnessing. We have both the authority and the power.

II. Part Two: *The Message*

A. The Basic Message (Christ)

1. Read I Corinthians 15:1-7.

a. Who is the center of the message?____________________

b. What are the basic facts about Christ? ____________________

1. This promise had special reference to the apostles but also applies to all Christians secondarily.

____

____

____

____

2. Read John 3:16-17.

   a. Who is Jesus? ______________________________

   b. What motivated God to send us Jesus? ______________

   ____

   c. What does God promise? ______________________

   ____

   d. What does God require man to do? ______________

Our message is not our experience but Christ—who He is and what He has done. To this we add the invitation to believe in Christ and be saved. This is the gospel. No matter what you tell a person, as long as you have not told him who Christ is and what Christ did in His death and resurrection, you have not witnessed for Christ. We are to offer Christ and the eternal life He brings to all on the condition of faith. Faith is more than intellectual assent; it is commitment of ourselves to Christ as our Lord.

B. Necessary Background Knowledge

A person may not be able to understand the gospel because he does not have a proper understanding of who God is and what man's problem is. When the apostles preached to Jews they could begin with Christ. However, when they preached to Gentiles they had to begin with who God is and what sin is. You also may need to start here when you witness.

Read Acts 17:22-31.

1. Where did Paul begin? (vv. 24-28) ________________

____

2. What did Paul tell the Athenians about God? ____________

____

____

____

____

3. What else does Paul discuss? (vv. 30-31) ____________________

____

____

Often it is necessary to tell people that the one *true* God is a God who is angry with man's sin. Today, many people do not believe they are sinners and do not believe God will judge them. You will need to tell them that God is entirely just and He will condemn men for their rebellion. Moreover, show them that they are sinners. Matthew 5:21-30 is a good passage with which to be familiar, as is Matthew 22:37-38. From here you can go on to show that Jesus is the only Savior. Knowing about God and their sin provides the basis for understanding Christ and the offer of life in Him. The following is a convenient summary of what to tell a person:

(1) God made us and will judge us.

(2) We have broken His laws and earned His punishment.

(3) Christ died for our sin and rose from the dead.

(4) We must trust in Christ as our Lord.

Here are the same four points in longer form. This four-point structure can be easily memorized as (1) God, (2) Man, (3) Christ and, (4) Faith:

(1) *God and Creation:* There is only one true God in three persons (Father, Son and Holy Spirit) who created and rules all things and who will judge all men.
(2) *Man and Sin:* Man was created to serve God, but we have rebelled against God by breaking His laws and so have brought condemnation and death upon ourselves.
(3) *Christ:* Christ is God's Son who became a man, died to pay the penalty for sin, arose from the dead, and now reigns forever.
(4) *God's Promise:* God promises to forgive all our sins, to adopt us as His children, to transform us into holy people, to resurrect

our bodies from the dead and to fellowship with us forever if we will turn away from our love of sin and trust in Christ as our risen Lord.

You can use Lesson One to review the basic content of these 4 steps.

III. Part Three: *The Method*

A. General Principles

1. Read Colossians 4:5-6.

a. What are you to be toward outsiders (unbelievers)? ____________

____

b. What should you make the most of? ______________________

____

c. What should your conversation be like? (v. 6) ______________

____

d. What should you know how to do? ______________________

____

2. Read I Peter 3:15-16.

a. What should be your attitude toward Christ? (v. 15)[2] __________

____

b. What should you be prepared to do? _____________________

____

c. In what way should you give answers? (v. 16) ______________

____

Our bearing witness for Christ must be a wise, gentle and loving thing. Mere volume is not what God wants. You must be gentle and wise, yet clear and uncompromising.

---

2. This means to enthrone Christ in your heart as your only and absolute Lord.

B. Some Specific Helps

There are essentially two kinds of people you can witness to: those you know, and strangers. You should begin your witnessing with the people you know. Then move on to contacting strangers. There are many ways to do this such as inviting people to your home for dinner or going door to door in your neighborhood. It is good to do this with another Christian. Your pastor can help you get started. Remember, look for opportunities to share Christ, and use them!

APPENDIX TO LESSON FOUR

HOW TO STUDY THE BIBLE

In some ways studying the Bible is like studying any book; in other ways it is unlike studying any other book. Because the Bible is written by men in human language the same rules of grammar, syntax and style apply to the Bible that apply to any human book. Yet the Bible is also *God's* Word so that, unlike any other book, it is without error, infallible and totally authoritative. Furthermore, the author of no other book lives in its believing readers as the Holy Spirit lives in every Christian. So then, Bible study must begin in prayer, for only the Holy Spirit can open our sin-blinded eyes to see and comprehend the message of Scripture. God the Holy Spirit will renew our hearts to receive and believe His words to us as we call upon Him in faith. Bible study will go nowhere unless there is a willingness to believe and obey all the Bible teaches. Again the Holy Spirit will give us hearts of love that are ready to obey the voice of the Spirit speaking in Scripture. However, since the Bible is in human words, we must be prepared to study hard. The Holy Spirit will not "whisper in our ear" the meaning of Scripture. Rather as we labor to understand the Bible, He will guide us into the truth. All the knowledge we need is in Scripture. The Spirit will open our hearts to receive that truth.

Basic Bible study can be divided into two parts: survey reading and intensive study. Survey reading is reading the Bible quickly in large segments to become familiar with its contents. Every Christian should read through the Bible at least once a year. (It takes only about 15 minutes a day.) Intensive study is when we study a smaller portion of the Bible (a book, paragraph or sentence) in depth. You cannot do this unless you are also reading the whole Bible in survey form. Otherwise you may very easily misinterpret the Bible passage because you are ignorant of other similar passages elsewhere. Both methods are needed and are complementary. If you are just starting to study the Bible, adopt a plan to read through the whole Bible (your Pastor can help) and set aside at least 15 minutes a day. Then choose an hour of one day somewhere else in the week for intensive study. The rest of this appendix will help you to do the intensive study.

Intensive study can also be divided into two methods: book study and theme study. Theme study is when you trace a theme or topic through all the books of the Bible. This is not the method for beginners to do on their own. However there are a variety of study guides that can help you. This study guide is a theme study. For your convenience, here are the basic rules for theme study: (1) Locate all the passages that deal with your topic (concordances are helpful for this). (2) Carefully study each passage. (3) Summarize the teaching of all of these passages and relate that summary to the whole of biblical teaching. So if you are studying God's love do not forget that God is also angry with His enemies.

Book study is the careful reading and reflection upon one book of the Bible. The basic rules are: (1) Read through the book once before beginning to study. (2) Divide the book into sections; then carefully study each section of the book and summarize the ideas. (3) Reread the whole book.

There are certain principles that must govern all our Bible study. These principles are just the consequences of the nature of the Bible as both a divine and a human book. First, always interpret Scripture by Scripture. (By the way, don't be scared by the word "interpret." Reading is always interpretation. It is not a matter of either interpreting the Bible or just reading it. Rather, it is whether my interpretation is true or false.) If there is an unclear passage, compare it with a clear one on the same topic. Scripture never contradicts itself, though our misinterpretations may collide. If you think a passage means "X" but you're sure the Bible elsewhere rejects such an idea, you need to see if you have misinterpreted the passage. Compare Scripture with Scripture and you will make great progress in Bible study.

The second principle is that you should interpret the Bible according to the grammar and syntax. This means, be sure it really says what you think it says. Don't read verses but whole sentences. (The verse numbers are human additions.) Don't read sentences without reading whole paragraphs. In other words, pay attention to how the words, sentences and paragraphs are put together. A sentence in its paragraph may mean something quite different from what you might think it means if it stands alone.

The third principle is to remember that the Bible was written by men who lived a long time ago. Their words reflect their culture and their times. This does not mean that the Bible is out of date. However, it does mean we must understand their words in the light of their culture and time. Be careful about seeing references to modern technological devices in the symbols of the Bible. Such references, if they were there, would be nonsense to the original writers and readers of the Bible.

For a good Bible study there are some helpful tools you need to buy. (Buy them slowly. They are absolutely indispensable!):

1. A concordance—(Young's or Strong's)
2. A Bible dictionary—(New Bible Dictionary, Davis' Bible Dictionary)
3. A book on Bible history—(DeGraaf's *Promise and Deliverance*)
4. A set of commentaries—(Calvin, Hendriksen, Tyndale, Henry)
5. A systematic theology book—(Berkhof)

APPENDIX TO LESSON TEN

SETTING UP A CONFERENCE TABLE[1]

PLACE

Agree upon an area in which daily conferences may be held without interruption. Choose a table, preferably one that is not used frequently for other purposes. Hold all conferences there. If problems arise elsewhere, whenever possible wait until you reach home to discuss them—at the conference table, of course. The first week read Ephesians 4:17-32 each night before conferring.

Place ______________________________

Time ________________________

PURPOSE

The conference table is a place to confer, not to argue. Begin by talking about yourself—your sins and failures—and settle all such matters first by asking forgiveness. Ask also for help (cf. Matthew 7:4-5).

Speak all the truth in love. Do not allow any concern to be carried over into the next day. Not all problems can be solved at one sitting. You may find it necessary to make up an agenda and schedule out the work over a period of time according to priorities. Direct all your energies toward defeating the problem, not toward the other person. Your goal is to reach biblical solutions, so always have Bibles on the table *and use them*. It helps to record the results of your work on paper. Open and close conferences with prayer. When you need help, reread Ephesians 4:25-32.

PROCEDURES

If any conferee argues, "clams up" or does anything other than confer at the table, the others must rise and stand quietly. This prearranged signal means, "In my opinion we've stopped conferring." Whether he was right or wrong in this judgment does not matter and ought not to be discussed at the moment. The person seated should then indicate his willingness to confer, and invite others to be seated again.

---

1. Copyright © 1980. Quantity supplies available; please write Christian Counseling & Educational Foundation, 1790 East Willow Grove Ave., Laverock, Pa. 19118.